EYEBALLS

PRIVATE EYE

First published in Great Britain 2012
by Private Eye Productions Limited
6 Carlisle Street London W1D 3BN

www.private-eye.co.uk

A catalogue record for this book is available
from the British Library.

ISBN 978-1-901784-58-9

Designed by Bridget Tisdall
Printed and bound in Great Britain by
Butler Tanner & Dennis, Frome, Somerset

MIX
Paper from
responsible sources
FSC® C023561

DUMB BRITAIN

EDITED BY
MARCUS BERKMANN

ILLUSTRATED BY
PENELOPE BEECH

INTRODUCTION

The Dumb Britain column has been running in Private Eye since 1997, collecting the daftest wrong answers given to quiz questions on radio and TV. After such a time, you would have thought the column's very existence would warn potential contestants of the perils of going on quiz shows when you don't know anything, but the ceaseless flow of Dumbs into the Eye's inbox suggests otherwise.

As this volume will show, The Weakest Link has proved our most fertile source for many years, and its cancellation briefly sent shivers through Carlisle Street. Happily, Bradley Walsh's ITV1 show The Chase has come to our rescue, with a brutal quickfire round that sorts the sheep from the goats and the goats from Dumb Britain entrants.

This collection also includes a handful of longer Dumbs not printed in the magazine, but gleaned directly from broadcasters who kept tapes of these things for their own private amusement. We would be delighted to hear from any other radio presenters or producers who would like to see their listeners' idiocies reproduced in future volumes. In the meantime, thanks to everyone who has contributed, and keep listening.

THE ABC

ANNE ROBINSON: Which B was one of the first two men to fly the Atlantic non-stop: Alcock and…?

CONTESTANT: Bull.

The Weakest Link, BBC1

PRESENTER: What 'G' is the national dish of Hungary?

CALLER: Goats.

BBC Radio Humberside

BRADLEY WALSH: What word is used for the letter 'B' in the phonetic alphabet?

CONTESTANT: Bob.

The Chase, ITV1

ANNE ROBINSON: What M, named after the Hebrew word for 'institution', is the national intelligence agency of Israel?

CONTESTANT: Al-Qaeda.

The Weakest Link, BBC1

GREG JAMES: Give me a word beginning with the letter N that's associated with winter.

CALLER: Moustache.

Radio 1

ANNE ROBINSON: In vocabulary, what 'O' is a word that specifically refers to a person between 80 and 89 years of age?

CONTESTANT: Old.

The Weakest Link, BBC1

ANNE ROBINSON: Which 'T' is the wife of Oberon and queen of the fairies in *A Midsummer Night's Dream*?

CONTESTANT: Tinkerbell.

The Weakest Link, BBC1

ANNE ROBINSON: Which R is a dish said to be best served cold?

CONTESTANT: Toast.

The Weakest Link, BBC1

ANNE ROBINSON: Which city in northern England is the only one that begins with the letter 'Y'?

CONTESTANT: Wakefield.

The Weakest Link, BBC1

ANNE ROBINSON: In Belgium, what Z is the name of the ferry port that's connected to the city of Bruges by a ship canal?

CONTESTANT: Zellweger.

The Weakest Link, BBC1

ANNE ROBINSON: In Britain, what three letters are used before the name of a man who has been knighted?

CONTESTANT: MBE.

The Weakest Link, BBC1

AMERICAN STUDIES

D.J. ROBERTO: What colour are the stars on the American flag?

CALLER: Blue… and, er, blue.

Capital FM, Manchester

ANNE ROBINSON: The motto of the FBI is 'Fidelity, Bravery...' and what?

CONTESTANT: Interrogation.

The Weakest Link, BBC1

ARCHITECTURE

ANNE ROBINSON: Which architect designed Terminal Five at Heathrow and the Welsh National Assembly building?

CONTESTANT (and eventual winner): Wren.

The Weakest Link, BBC1

ART

TERRY WOGAN: What colour is created by mixing red and yellow?

CONTESTANT 1: Green.

WOGAN: No, red and yellow.

CONTESTANT 2: Blue.

Wogan's Perfect Recall, C4

ANNE ROBINSON: Which American artist, influenced by comic strips, has the same surname as a small European principality?

CONTESTANT: Andy Warhol.

The Weakest Link, BBC1

BIOLOGY & NATURAL HISTORY

ANNE ROBINSON: In biology, what 'v' is the act of performing experiments on living animals?

CONTESTANT: Vasectomy.

The Weakest Link, BBC1

ANNE ROBINSON: A biped is a creature that walks on how many feet?

CONTESTANT: Five.

The Weakest Link, BBC1

TERRY WOGAN: What kind of animal doesn't change its spots?

CONTESTANT: Zebra.

Wogan's Perfect Recall, C4

ANNE ROBINSON: Which flower, found in a pond, rhymes with 'willy'?

CONTESTANT: Won't he.

The Weakest Link, BBC1

PRESENTER: Which dinosaur is named after the Greek for 'roofed lizard'? Is it barosaurus, stegosaurus or tyrannosaurus?

CONTESTANT: I'm going to go with tyrannosaurus.

PRESENTER: Do you think you're right?

CONTESTANT: I don't think I'm right at all.

PRESENTER: That's really an interesting strategy, to go for an answer you think is wrong.

CONTESTANT: I'm not blonde. I'm a woman with interesting hair.

Are You Smarter Than a Ten-Year-Old?

I'M NOT A TYRANNOSAURUS. I'M A STEGOSAURUS WITH RATHER SHORT ARMS. OKAY?

ANNE ROBINSON: The five breeds of swan found in the United Kingdom all have plumage of predominantly what colour?

CONTESTANT: Red.

The Weakest Link, BBC1

DICK OR DOM: What name is given to a male fox, a stag, a jack or a dog?

CONTESTANT: I think it's one of those three, isn't it?

Are You Smarter Than a Ten-Year-Old?

PRESENTER: Which dinosaur is named after the ancient Greek for 'three-horned face'?

CONTESTANT (a teacher): Right. You've got your Tyrannosaurus Rex. Or it could be that Pterodactyl type thing or something.

Are You Smarter Than A Ten-Year-Old?

DALE WINTON: Where does the common swift migrate to in the warm summer months?

CONTESTANT: I'm not sure what a common swift is. It's not a bird is it?

The National Lottery: In It To Win It, BBC1

ANNE ROBINSON: When people acquire a facial tan while wearing sunglasses, their eyes are sometimes said to resemble those of which rare Asian mammal?

CONTESTANT: Penguin.

The Weakest Link, BBC1

JOHN HUMPHRYS: Which insect gets its name from the ancient superstition that they crawled into people's ears while they were asleep?

CONTESTANT: Ants.

Mastermind, BBC2

CAREERS ADVICE

GREG JAMES: Name a job beginning with the letter Y.

CALLER: Yeti.

BBC Radio 1

CITIZENSHIP

BRADLEY WALSH: In which London palace was Queen Victoria born?

CONTESTANT: Crystal.

The Chase, ITV1

BRADLEY WALSH: Which of these dates came first in 2011: St George's Day, Easter Sunday or the Queen's real birthday?

CONTESTANT: Hmmm, St George's Day is the 23rd of April, isn't it?

WALSH: Er... er... I'll take your word for it.
The Chase, ITV1

JEREMY PAXMAN: What is the population density of the UK in persons per square kilometres? You can have 25 either way.

CONTESTANT: Three and a half.
University Challenge, BBC2

ANNE ROBINSON: Who is the father of Lady Sarah Chatto and Viscount Linley, the niece and nephew of the Queen?

CONTESTANT: Princess Anne.
The Weakest Link, BBC1

ANNE ROBINSON: In unusual pronunciations, the castle in Leicestershire that is home to the Duke of Rutland has a name that sounds the same as that of which animal?

CONTESTANT: Elephant.
The Weakest Link, BBC1

CLASSICS & ANCIENT HISTORY

ANNE ROBINSON: In Greek mythology, what was the name of the Titan who bore the weight of the world on his shoulders?

CONTESTANT: Anthrax.

The Weakest Link, BBC1

DALE WINTON: In Greek mythology, the principal gods lived on which mountain?

CONTESTANT: Well, I watch a lot of films, Dale, and there's a lot about Greek mythology with Thor and things like that in…

National Lottery: In It To Win It, BBC1

ANGUS PURDEN: According to legend, Romulus and Remus founded which city?

CONTESTANT: Edinburgh.

Postcode Challenge, STV

ANNE ROBINSON: The road known as Watling Street, which now incorporates part of the A5, was built by which ancient civilisation?

CONTESTANT: Apes.

The Weakest Link, BBC1

DOM OR DICK: Epeius was a master carpenter. What did he famously build for the ancient Greeks?

CONTESTANT: Erm, wasn't it that thing? It's like a building, with like, things? Pillars?

DICK OR DOM: We might be needing more of an answer than that.

CONTESTANT (rambles): A thing with pillars… The house of the gods…

Are You Smarter Than A Ten-Year Old

ANNE ROBINSON: In ancient history, Tutankhamun was king of which country?

CONTESTANT: Australia.

The Weakest Link, BBC1

MIKE PARRY: I'll give you the name and you give me the famous partner. OK?

CALLER: OK.

MIKE PARRY: So here goes. Antony and…?

CALLER: Dec.

TalkSPORT

DOMESTIC SCIENCE

GREG JAMES: Name a vegetable beginning with 'O'.

CALLER: Obergine.

Radio 1

ANNE ROBINSON: Catherine of Braganza, who was the wife of Charles I of England, popularised the drinking of which beverage in England?

CONTESTANT: Erm… Tequila Sunrise?

The Weakest Link, BBC1

JAMIE THEAKSTON: What do you do with edam and emmental?
CALLER: Put it in a sock.
Heart FM

D.J.: What animal do we get venison from?
CALLER: Snakes.
BRMB

ANNE ROBINSON: In America, what liquid normally comes out of a faucet?

CONTESTANT: Cheese.

The Weakest Link, BBC1

DRAMA

ANNE ROBINSON: Which musical, written in 1953 by Robert Wright and George Forrest, was set in medieval Baghdad?

CONTESTANT: South Pacific.

The Weakest Link, BBC1

DERMOT MURNAGHAN: In Shakespeare's play *Julius Caesar*, which character says, 'I come to bury Caesar, not to praise him'? Is it Cleopatra, Mark Antony or Brutus?

CONTESTANT: Well, I'm not sure, but I think it might be Brutus.

MURNAGHAN: Was that just a wild stab?

CONTESTANT: Yes.

Eggheads, BBC2

BRADLEY WALSH: Which Andrew Lloyd Webber musical concerns Juan Peron's wife?

CONTESTANT: Is it Cats?

The Chase, ITV1

ANNE ROBINSON: In *Hamlet*, a famous quotation is 'Get thee to a…' what?

CONTESTANT: Church on time.

The Weakest Link, BBC1

BRADLEY WALSH: A soliloquy is performed by how many people?

CONTESTANT: Four.

The Chase, ITV1

ECONOMICS

BRADLEY WALSH: Before decimalisation, a penny was represented by which letter of the alphabet?

CONTESTANT: a.

The Chase, ITV1

ANNE ROBINSON: Before decimalisation, how many shillings were there in a pound?

CONTESTANT: Three.

The Weakest Link, BBC1

ANNE ROBINSON: Since decimalisation in 1971, how many pennies have there been in a British pound?

CONTESTANT: Pass.

The Weakest Link, BBC1

HOST: What way does the profile of the Queen always face on a coin?

CALLER: Is it north?

Smooth Radio

ENGINEERING

ANNE ROBINSON: Nelson's flagship, the Victory, was built of which wood?

CONTESTANT: Balsa.

The Weakest Link, BBC1

ENGLISH LANGUAGE

ANNE ROBINSON: In cockney rhyming slang, the expression for 'road' is 'frog and…' what?

CONTESTANT: Pears.

The Weakest Link, BBC1

ANNE ROBINSON: Publicising a book on radio or TV is what, a plug or a bung?

CONTESTANT: Bung.

The Weakest Link, BBC1

ANNE ROBINSON: Which four-letter word is derived from the Arabic word for an upholstered seat with back and arms, for two or more people?

CONTESTANT: Chaise longue.

The Weakest Link, BBC1

ANNE ROBINSON: An Old Harrovian was a member of which famous public school?

CONTESTANT: Eton.

The Weakest Link, BBC1

PRESENTER: Complete the phrase, 'One in the hand is worth…?

CALLER: Two in the mouth?

Jack FM (Bristol)

ANNE ROBINSON: The phrase 'bareback riding' refers to riding without what?

CONTESTANT: Clothes.

The Weakest Link, BBC1

PRESENTER: What is a chaffinch?
CALLER: It's a measurement.
Heart FM (Bedfordshire)

ANNE ROBINSON: Which star sign is an anagram of 'spices'?
CONTESTANT: Scorpio.
The Weakest Link, BBC1

ANNE ROBINSON: In written communication, which country's name is an acronym for 'I trust and love you'?
CONTESTANT: Germany.
The Weakest Link, BBC1

DICK OR DOM: What is the pronoun in this sentence? 'The children asked if they could go on a picnic.'
CONTESTANT: I think it's 'asked'… It's either 'children' or 'picnic'… I'm going with 'children'.
Are You Smarter Than A Ten-Year-Old?

BRADLEY WALSH: Complete this well-known saying: 'To err is human, to forgive is…'
CONTESTANT: To forget?
The Chase, ITV1

DICK OR DOM: Is the verb in this sentence active or passive? 'A good goal was scored by Ronaldo.'

CONTESTANT: He scored so that's active to me. It's definitely active.

Are You Smarter Than A Ten-Year-Old?

DOM OR DICK: What is the suffix in this sentence? 'Millhouse was hopeful that he would get top marks in his exam.'

CONTESTANT: I'm not exactly sure what a suffix is. This is embarrassing. I work for a national newspaper.

DICK OR DOM: Which one?

CONTESTANT: *The Guardian*. I think it's 'exam'.

Are You Smarter Than A Ten-Year-Old?

ENGLISH LITERATURE

PRESENTER: Who wrote *A Tale Of Two Cities* and *Oliver Twist*?

CALLER: Eh?

PRESENTER: His first name was Charles.

CALLER: Shakespeare.

Heart FM (Cambridge)

ANNE ROBINSON: Which of these three –
heaven, hell or purgatory – is the subject of Dante's
Inferno?
CONTESTANT: Towering.
    The Weakest Link, BBC1

ANNE ROBINSON: In literature, *Untold Stories* is
the title of the 2005 memoir by which celebrated
English author and dramatist?
CONTESTANT: Shakespeare.
    The Weakest Link, BBC1

PRESENTER: What was the first name of the famous English poet Milton?

FIRST CALLER: Milton Keynes.

SECOND CALLER: Is it David?

THIRD CALLER: I haven't a clue.

FOURTH CALLER: I'm guessing Michael.

FIFTH CALLER: Oh, oh, we did him for 'A' level, all his works and that, but we never did his first name.

Radio City, Liverpool

DALE WINTON: What form of literature was Samuel Taylor Coleridge's 'The Rime of the Ancient Mariner'? Was it a novel, a stage play, or a poem?

CONTESTANT: A novel.

WINTON: It was a poem. I thought that 'rime' might be a clue.

CONTESTANT: I know. I thought it was a trick question.

National Lottery: In It To Win It, BBC1

ANNE ROBINSON: Gordon Brown compared himself to which literary character from Emily Brontë's *Wuthering Heights*?

CONTESTANT: Charles Dickens.

The Weakest Link, BBC1

PRESENTER: Who wrote the story of Peter Pan? A A Milne, J M Barrie or T S Eliot?

CONTESTANT (a teacher): Okay. I've read the story. I've saw the films. I've not saw the panto. I'm pretty sure it's T S Eliot.

Are You Smarter Than A Ten-Year-Old?

BRADLEY WALSH: In which century did the poet Geoffrey Chaucer live? Was it the 13th, the 14th or the 15th?

CONTESTANT: Well, I know he wrote one of Shakespeare's plays…

The Chase, ITV1

ANNE ROBINSON: Which book by Emily Brontë featured a character called Heathcliff?

CONTESTANT: Was it *Gone With The Wind*?

The Weakest Link, BBC1

ANNE ROBINSON: In English literary relationships, Mary Wollstonecraft Godwin, who wrote *Frankenstein*, married the poet Percy who?

CONTESTANT: Thrower.

The Weakest Link, BBC1

ANNE ROBINSON: Which boy's name precedes 'Sand' and 'Eliot' to make the pen-names of two 19th-century female authors?

CONTESTANT: Billy.

The Weakest Link, BBC1

ANNE ROBINSON: Which of these authors was female, T S Eliot or George Eliot?

CONTESTANT: T S Eliot.

The Weakest Link, BBC1

ANNE ROBINSON: In *Winnie the Pooh*, what type of animal is Tigger?

CONTESTANT: A rabbit.

The Weakest Link, BBC1

ANNE ROBINSON: *The Scarlet Pimpernel* was set during which revolution?
CONTESTANT: Industrial.

The Weakest Link, BBC1

ANNE ROBINSON: The ecclesiastical detective who featured in stories by G K Chesterton was known as Father…?

CONTESTANT: Ted.

The Weakest Link, BBC1

ANNE ROBINSON: Which London club was the start and finishing point of the journey in Jules Verne's novel *Around The World In Eighty Days*?

CONTESTANT (after a pause to think): Ronnie Scott's.

The Weakest Link, BBC1

ANNE ROBINSON: The humorous verses 'Oh I wish I'd looked after me teeth!' and 'They should have asked my husband' were written by which British poet?

CONTESTANT: Tennyson.

The Weakest Link, BBC1

ANNE ROBINSON: The American author of *The Secret History* and *The Little Friend* is Donna Tartt or Kebab?

CONTESTANT: Kebab.

The Weakest Link, BBC1

ANNE ROBINSON: Complete the quote by Oscar Wilde: 'I can resist anything except…'
CONTESTANT: Women.
The Weakest Link, BBC1

ANNE ROBINSON: The American author of travel books such as *Notes From A Small Island* and *A Walk In The Woods* is Bill…?
CONTESTANT: Shankly.
The Weakest Link, BBC1

FASHION

ANNE ROBINSON: The Canadian Mounted Police wear what type of hat, a stetson or a sombrero?

CONTESTANT: A sombrero.

The Weakest Link, BBC1

FILM STUDIES

ANNE ROBINSON: *Gone With The Wind* and *Rebecca* were both films produced by David O. … what?

CONTESTANT: Toole.

The Weakest Link, BBC1

ANNE ROBINSON: In the 1940s Laurence Olivier married which famous film star?

CONTESTANT: Mae West.

The Weakest Link, BBC1

MARRIAGE IS A FINE INSTITUTION, BUT I'M NOT READY FOR AN INSTITUTION

ANNE ROBINSON: In film comedy, the partner of Lou Costello was Bud who?

CONTESTANT: Holly.

The Weakest Link, BBC1

TERRY WOGAN: The title of the film that stars Nicole Kidman as Virginia Woolf is 'The…'?

CONTESTANT: Virginian.

Wogan's Perfect Recall, C4

JO RUSSELL: Which 1996 Leonardo di Caprio film was an adaptation of a famous Shakespeare play?

CALLER: Er… Titanic?

BRMB

ANNE ROBINSON: In 2006, the *Star Wars* character voted the most annoying film character ever was Jar Jar… what?

CONTESTANT: Gabor.

The Weakest Link, BBC1

ANNE ROBINSON: In film, the 2010 crime thriller adapted from a bestselling novel by Stieg Larsson was entitled *The Girl With The Dragon*…?

CONTESTANT: Teeth.

The Weakest Link, BBC1

GETHIN JONES: Which 1960s French actress and sex symbol has since founded an animal sanctuary?

CONTESTANT (after long deliberation): Marie Antoinette.

Sell Me The Answer, Sky 1

TOM DAVIES: What was the title of the last James Bond film?

CONTESTANT: Er…

DAVIES: It begins with a Q.

CONTESTANT: Qasino Royale.

Smooth Radio (north-east)

GAMES

BRADLEY WALSH: In the game of Cluedo, which character is coloured purple?

THE CHASER: Mrs Green.

The Chase, ITV1

ANNE ROBINSON: In sport, which phrase for a period of practice play before a tennis match is also a slang term for making someone pregnant?

CONTESTANT: Up the duff.

The Weakest Link, BBC1

ANNE ROBINSON: In England, how many teams normally contest a game of football?

CONTESTANT: Twelve.

The Weakest Link, BBC1

ANNE ROBINSON: The Barcelona footballer who won the Ballon d'Or in 2010 for the world's best player is Lionel... who?

CONTESTANT: Richie.

The Weakest Link, BBC1

DAVINA McCALL: What did Roger Bannister become the first man to do on this day in 1954? There are three possible answers, and they are: run the sub-four minute mile; go into outer space; put the toilet seat down.

ANDREW (broker, 26): He wasn't the first man in space.

VANESSA (dancer, 27): Put the toilet seat down?

ANDREW: Maybe. Maybe he invented the toilet seat. No, the toilet seat was Crapper. The man that invented the toilet seat was Crapper.

VANESSA: It didn't say he invented it. It said he put it down.

ANDREW: Yeah, yeah.

DAVINA: Fifty seconds.

VANESSA: Put the toilet seat down? Would that really have been a big thing?

ANDREW: Wait, wait. I think I've seen 'Bannister' on a toilet. Like a brand.

VANESSA: What are we going to do? Quick.

DAVINA: Twenty-five seconds.

VANESSA: Have you seen it, or not?

ANDREW: I think so, yeah.

VANESSA: I don't know.

ANDREW: Well, do you want to?

VANESSA: I don't know, I don't know. I don't know. Put it on there. I don't know.

[They put £50,000 on 'Put the toilet seat down'. Time's up.]

DAVINA: I just want to hug you two all the time. You are having no joy with these questions.

VANESSA: Who *knows* any of this?

The Million Pound Drop Live, Channel 4

PRESENTER: How many FA Cup final appearances has Ashley Cole made? Is it six or three?

CALLER: Four.

Breakfast show, TalkSPORT

TERRY WOGAN: What piece of clothing is traditionally awarded to a sportsman for representing his country internationally?

CONTESTANT (after long pause): A jockstrap?

Wogan's Perfect Recall, C4

BRADLEY WALSH: Due to his fast play, what is the nickname of snooker player Jimmy White?

CONTESTANT: Hurricane Higgins.

The Chase, ITV1

ANNE ROBINSON: This batsman was born in 1980 and made his debut for England in 2005. Kevin who?

CONTESTANT: Costner.

The Weakest Link, BBC1

BRADLEY WALSH: Shane Warne played Test cricket for which country?

CONTESTANT: France.

The Chase, ITV1

ALEXANDER ARMSTRONG: We gave one hundred people one hundred seconds to name as many first-class cricket counties as they could.

CONTESTANT: Twickenham.

Pointless, BBC1

ANNE ROBINSON: Three of the four Olympic throwing events are the discus, shot put and hammer. What's the other?

CONTESTANT: Long jump.

The Weakest Link, BBC1

GEOGRAPHY

ANNE ROBINSON: In which English county is the Cornish language spoken?

CONTESTANT: Devon.

The Weakest Link, BBC1

DERMOT MURNAGHAN: On which sea is the port of Le Havre: Mediterranean, English Channel or Adriatic?

CONTESTANT: It's not the English Channel for obvious reasons…

Eggheads, BBC2

ANNE ROBINSON: On an Ordnance Survey map, a pink triangle is used to denote what, a pyramid or a youth hostel?

CONTESTANT: A pyramid.

The Weakest Link, BBC1

JOHN HUMPHRYS: Tobermory is the chief town of which Hebridean island?

CONTESTANT: Sark.

Mastermind, BBC2

ANNE ROBINSON: Lancaster is the county town of which British county?

CONTESTANT: Lancastershire.

The Weakest Link, BBC1

DALE WINTON: The historic Stormont Castle is in the eastern part of which city?

CONTESTANT: Bristol.

National Lottery: In It To Win It, BBC1

ANNE ROBINSON: The coastal towns of Whitby and Scarborough lie next to which body of water?

CONTESTANT: The Atlantic.

The Weakest Link, BBC1

DALE WINTON: Which is the largest in area of the Canary Islands?

CONTESTANT: I know this. Jersey.

National Lottery: In It To Win It, BBC1

ANNE ROBINSON: What 'I' is a spa town in Yorkshire?
CONTESTANT: Innsbruck.
The Weakest Link, BBC1

ANNE ROBINSON: A popular coastal resort on the Bristol Channel is known as Weston-super-… what?
CONTESTANT: Market.
The Weakest Link, BBC1

ANNE ROBINSON: In which European country is the Neander valley?

CONTESTANT: Africa.

The Weakest Link, BBC1

ANNE ROBINSON: The Mississippi flows through almost the entire length of which country?

CONTESTANT: Egypt.

The Weakest Link, BBC1

ANNE ROBINSON: A peak in the Andes was confirmed by an expedition in 2000 as the source of which major river?

CONTESTANT: The Nile.

The Weakest Link, BBC1

ADRIAN DURHAM: What's the name of the river that runs through Rome?

CALLER: The Nile.

TalkSPORT

CHRIS MOYLES: Florence, from Florence and the Machine, is named after which Italian city?

CALLER: Rome.

Radio 1

BRADLEY WALSH: Which European capital city is divided into twenty arrondissements?

CONTESTANT: Sweden.

The Chase, ITV1

ANNE ROBINSON: A ship sailing south from Land's End in Cornwall will first hit land where?

CONTESTANT: Australia.

The Weakest Link, BBC1

JEREMY VINE: Florence Nightingale was born in which country: Italy, Austria or France?

CONTESTANT: There may be a clue in the name. Yes, I'll say France.

Eggheads, BBC2

ANNE ROBINSON: Talinn is the capital of which Baltic state?

LAW STUDENT: Spain.

The Weakest Link, BBC1

TERRY WOGAN: The Spanish Steps and the Colosseum lie in which Italian city?

CONTESTANT: Greece.

Wogan's Perfect Recall, Channel 4

ALEXANDER ARMSTRONG: We gave a hundred people a hundred seconds to name as many landlocked countries in Europe as they could.

CONTESTANT: I've been there twice, so I'm going to say Belgium.

CONTESTANT'S PARTNER (head in hands): We went by ferry.

Pointless, BBC1

ANNE ROBINSON: What is the easternmost destination on the Trans-Siberian railway?

CONTESTANT: Vienna.

The Weakest Link, BBC1

PRESENTER: What is the capital of Poland?

CALLER: Auschwitz.

PRESENTER: Did he just say that?

PRODUCER: Yes he did.

PRESENTER: Blimey.

Wire FM, Warrington

JEREMY PAXMAN: Work this out before you answer. The one-word correct English names of three EU member states end in the suffix 'land'. Ten points if you can name two of them.

CONTESTANT: Ireland and Swaziland.

University Challenge, BBC2

ANDREW CASTLE: In English, how many countries of the world have a name beginning with Q? None, one or two?

CONTESTANT 1: Quebec?

CONTESTANT 2: Yeah, Quebec. That's in South America, isn't it. Definitely Quebec.

Divided, ITV

NOEL EDMONDS: What is the highest layer of a rainforest called?

CONTESTANT: Well, at the bottom you've got grass and then it's shrubs and animals and things. So it's the trees.

Are You Smarter Than A Ten-Year-Old

ANNE ROBINSON: Which of these two shipping areas are in the North Sea: French Kiss or German Bight?

CONTESTANT: French Kiss.

The Weakest Link, BBC1

ANNE ROBINSON: Which range of mountains, running from Morocco to Tunisia, is named after a character in Greek mythology?

CONTESTANT: Gollum.

The Weakest Link, BBC1

ANNE ROBINSON: Which European country's name was literally intended to mean 'The Way North'?

CONTESTANT: America.

The Weakest Link, BBC1

ANNE ROBINSON: The name of which Canadian province is the Latin translation of 'New Scotland'?

CONTESTANT: Johannesburg.

The Weakest Link, BBC1

ALEXANDER ARMSTRONG: We gave one hundred people one hundred seconds to name as many states in the USA that have a coastline.

FIRST CONTESTANT (teacher): Mexico.

SECOND CONTESTANT (also a teacher): Orlando.

RICHARD OSMAN: The good news is that at least you're not a geography teacher.

Pointless, BBC1

ANNE ROBINSON: What is the name of the notorious island prison in San Francisco Bay that closed in 1963 and is now a top visitor attraction?

CONTESTANT: Guantanamo Bay.

The Weakest Link, BBC1

ANNE ROBINSON: Which South American country did cartoon character Homer Simpson mispronounce as 'You are gay'?

CONTESTANT: Bolivia.

The Weakest Link, BBC1

ANNE ROBINSON: The rivers East Dart and West Dart join to make the River Dart at a place called Dartmeet. In which English national park?

CONTESTANT (after long pause): Bodmin Moor.

The Weakest Link, BBC1

ANNE ROBINSON: Sofia is the capital of which central European country?

CONTESTANT: Bolivia.

The Weakest Link, BBC1

ANNE ROBINSON: North and South Korea are divided by the 38th what?

CONTESTANT: Step.

The Weakest Link, BBC1

MATHEMATICS

ANNE ROBINSON: What is 12 times six?
CONTESTANT: Pass.
   The Weakest Link, BBC1

ANNE ROBINSON: What is 20 minus eight?
CONTESTANT: Pass.
   The Weakest Link, BBC1

ANNE ROBINSON: What is 106 minus 75?
LAW STUDENT: Pass.
   The Weakest Link, BBC1

BRADLEY WALSH: From 1986, 1998 and 2004, you've picked 1998 as a leap year. That's a pure guess, isn't it?
CONTESTANT: Er… I just… I don't follow leap years. A day's a day, a year's a year, leap or no leap.
   The Chase, ITV1

ANNE ROBINSON: What's 80 percent of 200?
CONTESTANT: Four.
   The Weakest Link, BBC1

ANNE ROBINSON: What is 64 divided by eight?
CONTESTANT: Six.
 The Weakest Link, BBC1

JAMIE THEAKSTON: How many centimetres are
there in a metre?
CONTESTANT (confidently): Two and a half.
 Heart FM

ANNE ROBINSON: What number is represented by 10 to the power of three?

CONTESTANT: Six.

The Weakest Link, BBC1

ANNE ROBINSON: When counting down, what whole number follows 37?

CONTESTANT: Er, 19.

The Weakest Link, BBC1

DICK OR DOM: Express 55% as a fraction in its lowest possible form.

CONTESTANT: I can't think… five point… 50 per cent is one over two… one over 55… hang on! One over eleven… it's an eleventh.

Are You Smarter Than A Ten-Year-Old?

ANNE ROBINSON: What is 15 plus 17?

MATHS STUDENT: 33.

The Weakest Link, BBC1

NOEL EDMONDS: What is a twelve-sided solid figure called?

CONTESTANT: Well, I know ten sides is a hexagon. Or is it one of those tetra somethings?

Are You Smarter Than A Ten-Year-Old?

DICK OR DOM: Bob is building a wall 1.8 metres long. If each brick is 12 centimetres long, how many bricks will he need to complete the first row?

CONTESTANT: He's going to need a lot if he's building a wall.

Are You Smarter Than A Ten-Year-Old?

ANNE ROBINSON: What's the only prime number between 60 and 65?

CONTESTANT: 50.

The Weakest Link, BBC1

ANNE ROBINSON: What is the only prime number between 75 and 80?

CONTESTANT: 99.

The Weakest Link, BBC1

ANNE ROBINSON: How many days were there in 2008?

CONTESTANT (eventual winner): 322.

The Weakest Link, BBC1

ANNE ROBINSON: For what type of triangle might one use Pythagoras's theorem?

CONTESTANT: One with three points.

The Weakest Link, BBC1

DICK OR DOM: What does five squared equal?

CONTESTANT: In my day it was five times five, but I wonder if it may be the same as five cubed now.

Are You Smarter Than A Ten-Year-Old?

MEDIA STUDIES

CHRIS MOYLES: Who's the only original cast member on *EastEnders*?

CALLER (after some thought): Is it Rolf Harris?

BBC Radio 1

MELANIE SYKES: The TV show *The Merits of Ferrets* stars which type of animal?

CALLER: I don't know.

ALAN CARR: There's a clue, if you know where to look.

CALLER: I'm sorry, no.

SYKES (laughing): The answer is ferrets!

CALLER: Well how was I supposed to know that?

Allan Carr show, BBC Radio 2

EMMA FORBES: The programme *Inside John Lewis* is about which department store?

CALLER: Grace Brothers?

Allan Carr show, BBC Radio 2

ANNE ROBINSON: What was the surname of the former *Blue Peter* gardener nicknamed 'Percy Chucker' by Alan Titchmarsh?

CONTESTANT: Sledge.

The Weakest Link, BBC1

MARK GOODIER: *House*, *Jeeves And Wooster* and *Peter's Friends* all link which British actor?

CALLER: Oooh that's Hugh… erm…

GOODIER: Yep, that's it. Not a car or a van but a…?

CALLER: Bus?

Smooth Radio

ANNE ROBINSON: A national newspaper's name is shortened to 'the Indie'. Its sister publication has the nickname 'the Sindie'. On what day of the week is the Sindie published?

CONTESTANT: Wednesday.

The Weakest Link, BBC1

ANNE ROBINSON: Which Sunday newspaper once ran the headline, 'World War II Bomber Found On Moon'?

CONTESTANT: The Times.

The Weakest Link, BBC1

CHRISTIAN O'CONNELL: Of which Sunday newspaper was Andrew Neil once the editor?

CALLER: The Daily Star.

BBC Radio 5 Live

ANNE ROBINSON: Which long-running Radio 4 programme always begins with the words 'My castaway today is…'?

CONTESTANT: *The Archers.*

The Weakest Link, BBC1

ANNE ROBINSON: *La Stampa* and *La Repubblica* are newspapers published in which European country?

CONTESTANT: Mexico.

> *The Weakest Link, BBC1*

ANNE ROBINSON: Which 'Ian' edits *Private Eye*?

CONTESTANT: Himmler.

> *The Weakest Link, BBC1*

MEDICINE

BRADLEY WALSH: The hypothalamus is a part of which organ?

CONTESTANT: The pipes.

> *The Chase, ITV1*

ANNE ROBINSON: In medicine, a cochlear implant is designed to enhance which of the senses?

CONTESTANT: Can you repeat the question, please, Anne?

> *The Weakest Link, BBC1*

ANNE ROBINSON: The two cruciate ligaments in the knee are so named because they are shaped like what object?

CONTESTANT: A spoon.

The Weakest Link, BBC1

BRADLEY WALSH: What animal was formerly used by doctors to bleed patients?

CONTESTANT: Pigs.

The Chase, ITV1

MEDIEVAL HISTORY

ANNE ROBINSON: The first two Norman kings who ruled England in the latter part of the 11th century both had which first name?

CONTESTANT: Norman.

The Weakest Link, BBC1

PRESENTER: Which two counties fought the Wars of the Roses?

CALLER: Kent and Essex.

Magic FM

ANNE ROBINSON: One of the first major battles of the Hundred Years' War, fought in 1346, was the Battle of Crécy or Parsley?

CONTESTANT: Parsley.

The Weakest Link, BBC1

ANNE ROBINSON: In the early 15th century, Owain Glyndŵr led a rebellion against the ruling English in which country?

CONTESTANT: China.

The Weakest Link, BBC1

ANNE ROBINSON: In the Bayeux Tapestry, the character with the arrow in his eye is supposed to represent an English king with which first name?

CONTESTANT: I dunno. Er… George?

The Weakest Link, BBC1

MILITARY HISTORY

ANNE ROBINSON: Which organisation famously doesn't ask about the background of a new recruit, the Foreign Legion or the British Legion?

CONTESTANT: The British Legion.

The Weakest Link, BBC1

ANNE ROBINSON: The trumpet call of Reveille is a signal for soldiers to do what, wake up or start shooting?

CONTESTANT: Start shooting.

The Weakest Link, BBC1

MODERN HISTORY

DAMIAN WILLIAMS: Who was the first Tudor king?

CONTESTANT: I only know Henry VIII. He was a Tudor, but it sounds like he wasn't the first of anything. I wonder who his mum was? I'm going with Henry VIII.

Are You Smarter Than a Ten-Year-Old?

DICK OR DOM: What religion was Mary I?

CONTESTANT: She must have been before Henry VIII… I don't think she was Buddhist…

Are You Smarter Than A Ten-Year-Old?

ANNE ROBINSON: Which organ did Horatio Nelson lose at the Battle of Corsica?

CONTESTANT: Liver.

The Weakest Link, BBC1

ANGUS PURDEN: He was referred to as King James I in England. What was he called in Scotland?

CONTESTANT: George.

Postcode Challenge, STV

ANNE ROBINSON: The cape on which the Pilgrim Fathers landed in 1620 is named after which fish?

CONTESTANT: Haddock.

The Weakest Link, BBC1

ANNE ROBINSON: Lady Hamilton was the mistress of which famous British admiral?

CONTESTANT: Napoleon.

The Weakest Link, BBC1

PRESENTER: Where was Napoleon Bonaparte born?

CALLER: Was it England?

Heart FM

ANNE ROBINSON: Which American Civil War General had the nickname 'Stonewall'?

CONTESTANT: Custard.

The Weakest Link, BBC2

DERMOT MURNAGHAN: What's the common name of the small chamber in Fort William, Calcutta, that gained infamy in 1756?

C.J. DE MOOI: I'll try the Alamo.

Eggheads, G.O.L.D.

ANNE ROBINSON: Which country fought Germany in the Franco-Prussian War?

CONTESTANT: Spain.

The Weakest Link, BBC1

ANNE ROBINSON: In British history, although his real name was Albert, the king who succeeded his mother, Queen Victoria, in 1901 ruled under which other first name?

CONTESTANT: Albert.

The Weakest Link, BBC1

DERMOT MURNAGHAN: Which reigning British monarch spoke the following words on a radio broadcast? 'I have found it impossible to carry the heavy burden of responsibility and to discharge my duties as King as I would wish to do without the help and support of the woman I love.'

PhD HISTORY STUDENT: Er… there were a few Georges, weren't there? I'll say George IV.

Eggheads, BBC2

ANNE ROBINSON: In Ireland, the Easter Uprising of 1916: was it proclaimed from a post office or a betting shop?

CONTESTANT: A betting shop.

The Weakest Link, BBC1

ANNE ROBINSON: Who was the first King of England to speak on the radio?

CONTESTANT: Henry VIII.

The Weakest Link, BBC1

ANNE ROBINSON: In US history, during the Great Depression, parts of the midwest afflicted by drought and high winds became known as the what bowl?

CONTESTANT: Super.

The Weakest Link, BBC1

MARK GOODIER: Edward VIII abdicated the throne in order to marry whom?

CALLER: Anne Boleyn.

Smooth Radio

ANNE ROBINSON: Which monarch ruled Britain during the second world war?

CONTESTANT: George III.

The Weakest Link, BBC1

DALE WINTON: In 1962 the location of nuclear missiles on which island almost brought the USA and the USSR to war?

CONTESTANT: Easter Island comes to mind, but why would they go to war over Easter Island? I'm going to go for Hawaii.

The National Lottery: In It To Win It, BBC1

ANNE ROBINSON: The last German offensive of World War II in the Ardennes was known as the Battle of the… what?

CONTESTANT: Boyne.

The Weakest Link, BBC1

ANNE ROBINSON: The war between Israel and Egypt, which began on 5 June 1967 and ended on 10 June 1967, was better known by which name, based on its duration?

EVENTUAL WINNER: The ten-year war.

The Weakest Link, BBC1

ALEXANDER ARMSTRONG: In this round we're going to give you the names of some famous military events. We gave one hundred people one hundred seconds to tell us the conflict or war in which they occurred.

CONTESTANT: I've heard of Charge of the Light Brigade. So I'm going to go for that, and I'm going to say, World War One.

ARMSTRONG: OK. Very slight reaction from the audience there. Not sounding good, is it, James?

CONTESTANT: No.

RICHARD OSMAN: The over-fifties now throwing things at the television screen…

Pointless, BBC1

MODERN LANGUAGES

AL MURRAY: Which type of pottery takes its name from the Italian for baked earth?

FEMALE CONTESTANT: Lladro.

MURRAY: No.

MALE CONTESTANT: Royal Doulton?

Compete For The Meat, Dave

ANNE ROBINSON: Tolstoy wrote *War And Peace* in which language?

CONTESTANT: Latin.

The Weakest Link, BBC1

DERMOT MURNAGHAN: What is the official language of Mozambique?

CONTESTANT: Er… African?

Eggheads, BBC2

ANNE ROBINSON: In Russian literature, the author of Dr Zhivago was Boris what?

CONTESTANT: Karloff.

The Weakest Link, BBC1

ALEXANDER ARMSTRONG: We gave one hundred people one hundred seconds to name as many official languages of Switzerland as they could.

FIRST CONTESTANTS: Italian.

SECOND CONTESTANTS: Well, we think that could be wrong. So we'll go with a safe bet. English.

ARMSTRONG (deadpan): Safe bet. English.

Pointless, BBC1

MUSIC

ANNE ROBINSON: Which British composer wrote 'The Lark Ascending' and 'The Wasps Overture'?

CONTESTANT: Er… Beethoven?

The Weakest Link, BBC1

DOM OR DICK: What instrument represents the Duck in Prokofiev's *Peter And The Wolf*?

CONTESTANT: I'm trying to think which instrument looks like a duck.

Are You Smarter Than A Ten Year Old?

ANNE ROBINSON: A famous opera by Alban Berg is Lulu or Cilla?

CONTESTANT: Cilla.

The Weakest Link, BBC1

ANNE ROBINSON: Which ballet by Tchaikovsky is also the name of an instrument used to break open snacks such as almonds?

CONTESTANT: Hammer.

The Weakest Link, BBC1

ANNE ROBINSON: Gilbert and Sullivan's opera The Yeoman Of the Guard is set in which London landmark?

CONTESTANT: Canary Wharf.

The Weakest Link, BBC1

ANNE ROBINSON: Which country and western singer's biography is called 'Man In Black'?

CONTESTANT: Dolly Parton.

The Weakest Link, BBC1

PRESENTER: How many number ones have Take That had? Is it nine, seven or five?

CALLER: It's nine.

PRESENTER: Wrong, we'll ask the question again after this song. Phone in now.

[Plays song]

PRESENTER: So, how many number ones have Take That had? Is it nine, seven or five?

SECOND CALLER: I think the other caller said nine, didn't he.

PRESENTER: So what's your answer?

SECOND CALLER: Nine.

Lincs FM

D.J.: Name the 1970s group whose members were Graham Gouldman, Eric Stewart, Kevin Godley and Lol Creme.

CALLER: Crosby, Stills and Nash.

Smooth FM North East

PRESENTER: The reclusive Syd Barrett was a founder member of which group?

CALLER: Barrett Homes.

BBC Essex

ANNE ROBINSON: The man who gave his name to the musical version of *The War Of The Worlds* was called Jeff what?

CONTESTANT: Leppard.

The Weakest Link, BBC1

PRESENTER: Which Madonna song is also the name of a world-famous monthly magazine?

CONTESTANT: Like A Virgin.

Beauty And The Geek (US), ITV2

PAUL GAMBACCINI: W S Gilbert. What does the 'S' stand for in his name?

CONTESTANT: Humphrey.

Counterpoint, Radio 4

MYTH
&
LEGEND

D.J.: Which of these is one of Santa's reindeers:
Comet, Dixons or Currys?

CALLER: Dixons.

Heart FM

JOHN HUMPHRYS: Which legendary king owned a magic sword called Excalibur?

CELEBRITY: Herod.

Celebrity Mastermind, BBC1

DICK OR DOM: What did Old Mother Hubbard go to her cupboard to fetch?

CONTESTANT: Hmm… Old Mother Hubbard went to the cupboard to get herself a… It could have been a cup of coffee.

Are You Smarter Than A Ten Year Old?

PHILOSOPHY

ANNE ROBINSON: The French philosopher who said, 'Hell is other people,' is Jean-Paul… what?

EVENTUAL WINNER: Gaultier.

The Weakest Link, BBC1

POLITICS

MARK GOODIER: Name the Vince in charge of Business for the Coalition Government.

CALLER: Vince Hill?

Smooth Radio

ANNE ROBINSON: The MP and former GP was appointed Defence Secretary in May 2010 is Dr Liam…?

CONTESTANT: Gallagher.

The Weakest Link, BBC1

ANNE ROBINSON: Which Kate, a former Labour Minister for Sport, is now head of the Countryside Alliance?

CONTESTANT: Blanchett.

The Weakest Link, BBC1

ANNE ROBINSON: What was the name of the single issue party formed by Sir James Goldsmith in 1997 to fight that year's general election?

CONTESTANT: The Liberal Democrats.

The Weakest Link, BBC1

ANNE ROBINSON: The politician who, in 2004, had to pay over £12 million to Westminster Council because of the so-called homes-for-votes scandal was Dame Shirley who?

CONTESTANT: Bassey?

The Weakest Link, BBC1

ANNE ROBINSON: In the 1960s, one of the figures at the centre of the political scandal known as The Profumo Affair was Christine who?

CONTESTANT: Hamilton.

The Weakest Link, BBC1

ANNE ROBINSON: The phrase 'Workers of the World Unite' in inscribed on the tomb of which political thinker in Highgate Cemetery, north London?

CONTESTANT (without hesitation): Enoch Powell.

The Weakest Link, BBC1

ANNE ROBINSON: Karl Marx described what as the opium of the people: television or religion?

CONTESTANT: Television.

The Weakest Link, BBC1

ALEXANDER ARMSTRONG: We gave one hundred people one hundred seconds to name as many post-war Conservative Chancellors of the Exchequer as they could.

CONTESTANT: Right. The only one… I'm not sure whether he was Conservative… is Gordon Brown.

Pointless, BBC1

ANNE ROBINSON: The Speaker of the House of Commons between 1983 and 1992, and the last to wear the traditional full wig, was Bernard…?

CONTESTANT (after some thought): Manning.

The Weakest Link, BBC1

ALEXANDER ARMSTRONG: We gave one hundred people one hundred seconds to name as many alliteratively named US Presidents as they could. Richard?

RICHARD OSMAN: Yes, in the history of the US Presidency, from 1789 all the way up to 2010, there have been four US Presidents whose first name and surname started with the same letter. We're looking for the most obscure of those.

CONTESTANT: I think we've decided.

ARMSTRONG: OK.

CONTESTANT: Lyndon Johnson.

Pointless, BBC1

ANDREW CASTLE: How many MPs are there in the House of Commons?

CONTESTANT: I don't know what the House of Commons is… I think it's something to do with politics.

Divided, ITV1

ALEXANDER ARMSTRONG: We gave one hundred people one hundred seconds to name as many Prime Ministers or Presidents of the Republic of Ireland since 1937 as they could. You have to come up with three of them.

CONTESTANT 1: I don't know why Neil Kinnock seems to spring to mind, but he's probably someone totally different.

CONTESTANT 2: I'm staying quiet.

CONTESTANT 1: I really can't think of anyone else right now.

CONTESTANT 2: We'll just have to make names up.

ARMSTRONG: I am going to need three names from you.

CONTESTANT 1: I'm going to go for Neil Kinnock.

CONTESTANT 2: I'm going to go for Paddy because that's a popular first name, and Ashdown, and I know that's wrong.

CONTESTANT 1: This is probably really ignorant, the one I'm about to say, because he might be Scottish, so I'm really sorry about this if I have offended anyone, but Tony... Benn?

Pointless, BBC1

ANNE ROBINSON: Which southern European country was ruled by Antonio Salazar from 1932 to 1968?

CONTESTANT (certain): Russia.

The Weakest Link, BBC1

ANNE ROBINSON: Juan Peron was twice the President of which South American country?

CONTESTANT: Poland.

The Weakest Link, BBC1

ANNE ROBINSON: Which Mikhail was the last head of state of the Soviet Union?

CONTESTANT: Lenin. Mikhail Lenin.

The Weakest Link, BBC1

ANNE ROBINSON: When the Prime Minister calls a general election, he runs to the hills or goes to the country?

CONTESTANT: Runs to the hills.

The Weakest Link, BBC1

ANNE ROBINSON: For which party did Caroline Lucas win their first ever seat at the 2010 general election?

CONTESTANT (after much thought): Labour.

The Weakest Link

JEREMY PAXMAN: Which Swiss ski resort hosts an annual summit of global political and economic leaders?

CONTESTANT: Davros.

University Challenge, BBC2

RELIGIOUS EDUCATION

ANNE ROBINSON: What is the name of the Archbishop of Canterbury who compiled the first Book of Common Prayer?

CONTESTANT: Samuel Pepys.

The Weakest Link, BBC1

ANNE ROBINSON: After his resurrection, Jesus appeared to two of his disciples on the road to where – Emmaus or Amarillo?

CONTESTANT (after some consideration): Amarillo.

The Weakest Link, BBC1

JOHN HUMPHRYS: In which language was the Koran written?

CONTESTANT: German.

Mastermind, BBC2

ANNE ROBINSON: In the New Testament, it's said to be easier for which animal to go through the eye of a needle, than for a rich man to enter the kingdom of God?

CONTESTANT: Is it a mouse, Anne?

The Weakest Link, BBC1

DICK (OR DOM): How many sons did Noah have: three, five or eight?

CONTESTANT: Oh my god, I have no idea. I thought Noah had the Ark. I didn't know he had sons.

Are You Smarter Than A Ten-Year Old

ANNE ROBINSON: The traditional wording of the Lord's Prayer asks that we be delivered from… what?

CONTESTANT: Our daily bread.

The Weakest Link, BBC1

ANNE ROBINSON: Which name for a building used by members of the Jewish faith is derived from a Greek word that means 'an assembly'?

CONTESTANT: Mosque.

The Weakest Link, BBC1

ANNE ROBINSON: The ten-yearly gathering of Anglican bishops hosted by the Archbishop of Canterbury is known as the Lambeth what?

CONTESTANT: Walk.

The Weakest Link, BBC1

SCIENCE

BRADLEY WALSH: Which Soviet space station was launched in 1986?

CONTESTANT: Sputnik.

The Chase, ITV1

TOM NEWITT: Who was the first man in space?

CONTESTANT: Christopher Columbus.

Beacon Radio

JEREMY PAXMAN: When Neil Armstrong said in 1969 that the surface of the moon felt like crunchy snow underfoot, he was confirming a prediction made in 1964 by which Dutch-born US astronomer?

CONTESTANT: Patrick Moore.

University Challenge, BBC2

BRADLEY WALSH: Which barrier was smashed by Chuck Yeager in the X-1 rocket plane?

CONTESTANT: The Thames Barrier.

The Chase, ITV1

BRADLEY WALSH: Who devised the Centigrade scale?

THE CHASER: Fahrenheit.

The Chase, ITV1

ANNE ROBINSON: Which 19th century chemist was invited to join the Royal Society after discovering the anaesthetic properties of nitrous oxide?

CONTESTANT: Boots.

The Weakest Link, BBC1

GETHIN JONES: What is the more common name given to the aurora borealis?

CONTESTANT: Hmm. I'm not really a plant person.

Sell Me The Answer, Sky Two

ANNE ROBINSON: Vulcanisation improves the strength of rubber by adding which non-metallic element?

EVENTUAL WINNER: Wool.

The Weakest Link, BBC1

DALE WINTON: What gas has the chemical symbol CO_2?
CONTESTANT: Petrol.
   National Lottery: In It To Win It, BBC1

DJ ALLY BAILLY: Who was the first woman, in 1903, to be awarded a Nobel Prize for her work on radioactivity?
CALLER: Florence Nightingale.
   Radio Clyde

THE LADY IS THE LAMP

MULTIPLE CHOICE

ANNE ROBINSON: In modern slang, what is a soap dodger: someone who doesn't wash, or someone who avoids watching *EastEnders*?

CONTESTANT: Someone who avoids *EastEnders*.

The Weakest Link, BBC1

ANNE ROBINSON: Does the word 'tonsorial' refer to hairdressing or cross-dressing?

CONTESTANT: Cross-dressing.

The Weakest Link, BBC1

ANNE ROBINSON: If something is fossilised in stone, is it terrorised or petrified?

CONTESTANT: Terrorised.

The Weakest Link, BBC1

ANNE ROBINSON: Beethoven and Schubert: were they bachelors or bigamists?

CONTESTANT: Bigamists.

The Weakest Link, BBC1

ANNE ROBINSON: Custom tailoring is called bespoke or beheard?

CONTESTANT: Beheard.

The Weakest Link, BBC1

I'M A CELEBRITY, GET ME OUT OF DUMB BRITAIN

JOHN HUMPHRYS: Which classic sparkling wine is named after the region of north-eastern France where it originated?

STACEY SOLOMON: Erm… I dunno… er…

JOHN HUMPHRYS: Sparkling wine?

STACEY SOLOMON: Jacob's Creek.

Celebrity Mastermind, BBC1

JOHN HUMPHRYS Which political doctrine mentioned in the title of Karl Marx's 1848 manifesto seeks to replace private property and a profit-based economy with public ownership?

WAYNE HEMINGWAY: Mein Kampf.

Celebrity Mastermind, BBC1

JOHN HUMPHRYS: Which popular pizza, that shares its name with a famous work by Vivaldi, is normally divided into four sections, each containing different toppings?

SNOOKER'S JOHN HIGGINS: Four cheeses.

Celebrity Mastermind, BBC1

JOHN HUMPHRYS: The 15th-century dynastic struggle known as the Wars of the Roses were fought between the House of Lancaster and which other royal House?

RICHARD ARNOLD: The Stuarts! The Tudors! Aaaarrgh!

Celebrity Mastermind, BBC1

JOHN HUMPHRYS: In the United States a patent was granted to Alexander Graham Bell on March 7th, 1876, for which invention?

STACEY SOLOMON: The lightbulb.

Celebrity Mastermind, BBC1

VERNON KAY: Name something a bald man doesn't need to buy.

BOBBY DAVRO'S DAD: A razor.

All-Star Family Fortunes, ITV

JOHN HUMPHRYS: Which famous detective made his first appearance in the story 'A Study In Scarlet'?

SASCHA KINDRED: Columbo.

Celebrity Mastermind, BBC1

PhD

DANNY KELLY: In braille, which letter consists of a single dot?

CALLER: One.

KELLY: One's not a letter. Is it? Let me just check with the producer. No, one is definitely not a letter.

CALLER: Three.

KELLY: No, three's not a letter. One to ten aren't letters. Which letter consists of a single dot?

CALLER: It'll be four.

KELLY: Sorry, can you give me that answer again?

CALLER: Four.

KELLY: Let me read out the question once again. In braille, which letter consists of a single dot? And as I was just saying, it tends not to be a number.

CALLER: [thinking]

KELLY: You've gone for one, three and four. What would you like to go for next?

CALLER: Er… three.

BBC Radio WM

DANNY KELLY: Where is the cornea?

CALLER: Where is where?

KELLY: Where is the cornea? C-O-R-N-E-A.

CALLER: Don't know.

KELLY: You don't know?

CALLER: No.

KELLY: So do you want to play your joker? [And get a clue.]

CALLER: Yeah.

KELLY: If you play darts, what do you get 50 for? Where do you have to get the dart on the dartboard to get 50?

CALLER: The bullseye.

KELLY: Yeah. So, now you know that, where's the cornea?

CALLER: Bullseye. Er, 25.

KELLY: No, the bullseye is 50.

CALLER: Yeah. 25. Yeah.

KELLY: So the cornea is…

CALLER: 25.

KELLY: No, it's on the body, on the human body. So where's the cornea?

CALLER: On the board. By the bullseye.

KELLY (laughs): No.

CALLER: 25.

KELLY: It's nothing to do with bloody darts.

CALLER: Isn't it?

KELLY: No, no. The clue there was bullseye. It's actually on the body. So where's the cornea?

CALLER: 25.

KELLY: Do you work, Gareth?

CALLER: Yeah, I do, yeah.

KELLY: What do you work as?

CALLER: Scaffolder.

KELLY: Any scaffolding ever fallen on your head?

CALLER: Not yet.

KELLY: Whereabouts on your body would you have a cornea?

CALLER: On me head.

BBC Radio WM

'Of course in days gone by, it wasn't unknown for Djokovic to be injured in the big matches. Fatally injured.'

SIMON REED

THOUGHT FOR THE DAY

'I went to church, religiously.'
DENISE LEWIS

'I think it was nerves that made me nervous.'
ANDY MURRAY

'In four letters, it sucks!'
JEFF TARANGO

'Flushing Meadows by night is a glorious sight.
There are 23,700 spectators packed into every seat.'
RADIO 5 LIVE

'You need luck on the way and he [Andy Murray]
got dealt a little short end of the stick.'
JOHN McENROE

'Roddick tried to hold the mantelpiece for
American tennis.'
GREG RUSEDSKI

'That match is already being hailed as one of the
all-time greats of last year.'
JOHN LLOYD

'In what other sport do you play six hours of
tennis?
GREG RUSEDSKI

'I don't know who fist-pumps more, Maria [Sharapova] or Sacha, her fiancé.'
LINDSAY DAVENPORT

'If you let Rafa get on top of you, he's like an express train.'
SUE BARKER

'Well, it's a brighter day today than it was yesterday. At least, it was before it got dark.'
JONATHAN OVEREND

TENNIS

'The way he looks on a tennis court, the way he looks on a practice court, I'm sure the way he looks in the shower too. He is not a big man, but he has a big weapon.

> *MATS WILANDER*

'His [Andy Murray's] balls are 10 to 15 per cent heavier now than at the start…'

> *JEFF TARANGO*

'Federer's balls look like watermelons out there.'

> *BORIS BECKER*

'He has Del Potro on the back seat.'

> *BORIS BECKER*

'I think it's amazing we have four players in the semi-final.'

> *ANNABEL CROFT*

'She [Date-Krumm] must have reactions like those Top Cat fighter pilots.'

> *DAVID MERCER*

'I'm going to put the cat amongst the feathers.'
STAN COLLYMORE

'Kyrgiakos has gone, and Jamie Carragher isn't getting any older.'
STAN COLLYMORE

'I don't hate Arsenal. "Hate" isn't a word that's in my vocabulary.'
STAN COLLYMORE

'Whatever it is that he's got, he's got it.'
STAN COLLYMORE

SPEAKING THE LANGUAGE

'That basic skill of articulacy should be better trained into them…'

SIMON HEFFER

'I think he's really nailed the inarticulessness.'

LOUISE DOUGHTY

'He [Carlos Tevez] has been in England for five years now. So it's disappointing that his English isn't as good as what it should be…'

GRAHAM TAYLOR

STAN

'If my gran had had cojones, she'd have been my uncle.'

STAN COLLYMORE

'Roy Hodgson has only just got his feet under the door…'

STAN COLLYMORE

'Yes, that was unlucky for Judd Trump. Before the tournament he was the favorite to pick up a bout of food poisoning'
KEN DOHERTY

'I've never said the word "never".'
BARRY HEARN

'Trump is like a breath of fresh air.'
JOHN VIRGO

'This young man [Judd Trump] is on the precipice of greatness.'

KEN DOHERTY

'If it wasn't for gravity, that red would never have dropped into the pocket.'

NEAL FOULDS

NEWTON DISCOVERS SNOOKER

'Shingler and his brother both have a mother in Dumfries.'
> *ANDREW COTTER*

'They [the Welsh] have got the boat back on the road.'
> *IAN ROBERTSON*

'Either you score or you don't from that position.'
> *BRIAN MOORE*

'He's seized this game by the scruff of his teeth.'
> *JAMES BURRIDGE*

SNOOKER

'Matthew Stevens got a terrible kick in the balls and it cost him his last-16 match…'
> *JOHN PARROTT*

'It was like the Sea of Galilee there, the reds just parted and the pink was available.'
> *WILLIE THORNE*

'There goes Vainikolo with his hair up to the halfway line…'

ESPN

'Bergamasco was breathing right down Conor Murray's throat again there.'
> *NICK MULLINS*

'France are always capable of pulling the hat out of the bag.'
> *JOHN GALLAGHER*

'He's struck that straight between the middle.'
> *PHIL VICKERY*

'I won't ask you to name any highlights from your great career… but what was the best moment?'
> *SONJA MCLAUGHLAN (to Shane Williams)*

'Brian Moore's World Cup medal is floating somewhere at the bottom of the Thames.'
> *JEFF PROBYN*

'Graeme Morrison, on the touchline. You're getting a real bird's eye view, down there at ground level.'
> *BBC RADIO SCOTLAND*

ROYALS

'Should Fergie be invited to the wedding? Her kids will be there, Beatrice and Potter.'
SADIE NINE

'William and Kate will consummate their relationship tomorrow in the Abbey.'
RICHARD MADELEY

RUGBY

'That try is going to make no difference to the score.'
LAWRENCE DALLAGLIO

'They are there to wrong the right of the last World Cup…'
JENNY SUTTON

'It's 50-50 in Wales's favour.'
IAN ROBERTSON

'I find her incredibly credible.'
KARREN BRADY, The Apprentice

'Never look a gift horse in the eye.'
DUANE BRYAN, The Apprentice

'Don't these people realise this is reality TV. It's not really real.'
ALED JONES

'This is all about courage, whether you've got the balls to actually smell what is going on in business.'
ALAN SUGAR, The Apprentice

'I think it's an opportunity for them [young unpaid interns] to be punctual, to be reliable, to learn work skills and then to go on and go into full-time unemployment.'

PAUL NUTTALL

REALITY

'You were so far up Jim's behind, you couldn't see the wood for the trees.'

NATASHA SCRIBBINS, The Apprentice

'No tax rate should be set in stone. I don't want to see any taxes higher than we can avoid.'
ED BALLS

'I didn't come into politics to cut public sponging…'
NICK CLEGG

'We must take care not to choke off the recovery at the knees.'
FRANCIS MAUDE

'We have inherited a huge problem on obesity.'
ANNE MILTON

'The situation is not black and white as it was in South Africa.'
PETER HAIN

'We've got to wait until all the facts of the case are known before we jump to conclusions.'
PHILIP HAMMOND

'Everyone is innocent until presumed guilty.'
SIR MENZIES CAMPBELL

'I'm not going to sit in judgement, standing here...'

ED MILIBANDV

'These books didn't need to stand on Denis's shoulders. They could stand on their own shoulders...'

SHIRLEY WILLIAMS

'Ken [Livingstone] is a Marmite character – you either love him or loathe him or shades in between.'

TESSA JOWELL

PER CENT

'Number one for us is giving 110 per cent, and
nine times out of ten we do.'
MICHAEL KIGHTLY

POLITICS

'Well, Eamonn, that's not the picture I'm hearing.'
BRENDAN BARBER

'Victories always hurt more when you lose'
  MARK FOSTER

'This (pointing to head) is the biggest brain in your body!'
  CLARE BALDING

'That could be the leg that keeps her on the podium'
  SHIRLEY ROBERTSON

'It's not often you get a once-in-a-lifetime opportunity'
  NICK DEMPSEY

'Oh and the Austrians are confused… the Australians, I beg your pardon, are confused'
MATT CHILTON

'He's saying something but unfortunately I can't lipread Austrian'
CANOEING COMMENTATOR

'He literally cut Craig Bellamy in half'
MICKY QUINN

'We can catch the wave and run with it'
STEVE BACKLEY

'All you can say is sometimes you love sport, and sometimes you hate sport, but basically you love it'
JOHN INVERDALE

'[Andy Murray] has forced Federer into the unforced errors'
TIM HENMAN

'What characteristics make a good cox? Obviously the size has to be right'
SUZIE FOWLER-WATT

'Swimmers are swimming fifteen to seventeen thousand kilometres a day'
SWIMMING EXPERT, Sky Sports News

'Drama from start to beginning'
MICHAEL TUCKER

'The crowd literally carried us round the course'
WILLIAM FOX-PITT

'And today, at the Olympics, we have the men's cockless fours'
NEWSREADER, JAZZ FM

OLYMPICS

'But it might not be Usain Bolt's body but his mind that's the problem,' said the Jamaican team's head doctor'
  KEME NZEREM

'I never dreamed I would be the flag-bearer. So, yeah, it's a dream come true'
  CHRIS HOY

'I was thumbing through the dictionary last night, trying to see if there are other words than "amazing, extraordinary, remarkable". I'm not sure there are'
  JOHN INVERDALE

'That performance has left us speechless. Let's talk about it'
  ANDY JAMESON

'This is the smoking mirror of cycling'
  MICHAEL HUTCHINSON

'Mistakes will be made tonight, make no mistake'
  GARTH CROOKS

'How about people with implants if the company that supplied them has gone bust?'
      JUSTIN WEBB

'And it comes with a caveat that could be read as a warning.'
      ANITA ANAND

'David Cameron is an excellent communicator, but it's not always easy to understand what he's trying to communicate.'
      MATTHEW PARRIS

'It gives us a bit of a barometer of the political temperature right now in Zimbabwe.'
> *STEVE VICKERS*

'George Osborne is under attack from Tory backbenders… er, backbenchers.'
> *LBC*

'My memory of the time – and we're talking about the early part of next year…'
> *ADAM BOULTON*

'Is the gunman thought to be armed?'
> *VICTORIA DERBYSHIRE*

'Mr Balls, it's not a hypothetical: if you were in charge tomorrow, what would you do?'
> *KIRSTY WARK*

'Half the unemployed people in Spain are without work.'
> *LOUISE COOPER*

'Police enquiries into child abuse is in its infancy.'
> *CHRIS BUCKLER*

'And we still don't know where some of the missing are.'

> *JOHN KING (on the Costa Concordia sinking)*

'Conditions at Heathrow have been exasperated by freezing fog.'

> *KEITH DOYLE*

'We're all going to die at least once.'

> *EVAN DAVIS*

'These new tests are making disabled people jump through hoops.'
   RADIO 2

'You had an accident when you were 21, when you were hit by a car. What impact did that have on you?'
   JENNI MURRAY

'When Andy Coulson, as it were, bit the bullet, fell on his sword and stood down…'
   STEVE HEWLETT

'People can come along and spend a little time with Jimmy [Savile] in his coffin.'
   BBC1

[During rescue of fifth Chilean miner] 'There he is, bright-eyed. Except for the sunglasses.'
   ANDREW WILSON

'It has been confirmed the body of Colonel Gaddafi will be buried in a secret location, although it is not yet clear where.'
   BBC 6 MUSIC

'When dealing with flood matters, I prefer to see a problem as a glass half-full rather than one half-empty.'

   SPOKESMAN, Flood Defence Agency

'He hides his academic bushel under a shrewd carapace.'

   PAT MURPHY

'If a footballer presents himself as a family man and goes and has sex with a prostitute, should he gag her?'

   NICKY CAMPBELL

'Hugh Grant is still sore after reports about his meeting a prostitute.'

   ADAM BOULTON

'There's a lot of beating around the bush.'

   ARIANNE COHEN on how British women talk about their sex lives

'It's great that there's greater awareness about Alzheimer's, which is almost the forgotten disease.'

   BILLY BUTLER

'The remains of Shackleton's number two can be found on South Georgia.'
BBC WORLD SERVICE

'Cracks began to appear when rival publications began to show much more explicit photos…'
RADIO 4

NEWS & COMMENT

'It's been announced that Northern Rock has been sold to Virgin Mary.'

PETER ALLEN

'They need to put their best foot forward and make a good fist of it.'

TODAY PROGRAMME

'There's going to be an influx of poorer Londoners fleeing London.'

VANESSA FELTZ

'There are people alive now who lost their lives in the fight for Irish freedom.'

RADIO 5 LIVE

'Today's news is yesterday's fish and chip papers, as the saying goes.'

ALAN YOUNG

'He's not going to be the white horse on the charger.'

STEPHANIE FLANDERS

MUSIC

'I'm not stupid – I've read Smash Hits since I was 12 years old.'

>*MARK FEEHILY (of Westlife)*

'She's going to be playing a few gigs in her home town of Devon.'

>*FEARNE COTTON*

'A man who recently celebrated half a decade in the business: Cliff Richard.'

>*ITV3*

'Don't wanna kill myself – been there and done that before and it makes me miserable.'

>*CLAIRE RICHARDS (of Steps)*

'All weekend I've been struggling with a nervous rear end.'

JENSON BUTTON

'He drives with the seat of his pants.'

EDDIE JORDAN

'The rider [Shoya Tomizawa] passed away, so we wish him, his team, his family, the very best…'

JENNY GOW

'And Lewis Hamilton has won the Chinese Grand National…'

RADIO 4 NEWSREADER

MORON

'You were once voted the greatest living artist, beating Rembrandt and Constable.'
PIERS MORGAN (to Rolf Harris)

MOTOR SPORT

'This is where Massa had his terrifying accident last year. In fact you can still see the skidmarks.'
MARTIN BRUNDLE

'That was Sebastian Vettel nearly going into the back of one of the virgins.'
DAVID COULTHARD

'Kobayashi's just a sitting duck, and in two quacks of a duck's tail he's out of the way.'
DAVID CROFT

'I am the first of the losers, which is better than anyone else.'
LEWIS HAMILTON

'The England team literally cut the mould off the cheese.'

CALLER, Radio 5 Live

'He [Usain Bolt] had hordes of South Koreans quite literally on a piece of string.'

MARK POUGATCH

'She literally pulled the hatches down and locked the doors with 50 metres to go.'

KATHARINE MERRY

'And Förstemann has a problem now. His opponent, Sir Chris Hoy, is literally on fire.'

HUGH PORTER

'Lokomotiv are literally putting bodies on the line.'

CLIVE TYLDESLEY

'In Sweden they literally split the child in half to spend time with each parent.'

ULRIKA JONSSON

'It literally catapulted him to fame.'

JANE JONES

LITERALLY

'It's up in the mountains, literally at the epicentre of nowhere…'
   CHARLIE COX

'There was literally two heads on me, I had literally two heads…'
   LAURA MOORE

'Hamilton literally throwing that McLaren around…'
   MARTIN BRUNDLE

'The boys' performance today was so good, I've literally run out of expletives to describe it.'
   MICKY MELLON

'Whenever she had any good opportunities, my daughter literally shot herself in the foot.'
   VIDAL SASSOON

'Pakistan placed a fielder at square leg for the attempted hook, and Pietersen literally hit it straight down his throat'
   JONATHAN AGNEW

'And of course Andy [Carroll], when he had to open his legs and provide us with a target, then he did do.'

CHRIS HUGHTON

'They've almost won the game at a canter without using any of their legs.'

GARY NEVILLE

'Some of these kids would give their right leg to become a professional footballer.'

DARREN GOUGH

'The Manchester United players are very misgruntled with that decision.'
MARK LAWRENSON

'He [Daniel Sturridge] was onside because he wasn't offside.'
MARK LAWRENSON

'Everyone says he's stubborn, and he is stubborn. But is he stubborn, Ian?'
MARK LAWRENSON

LEGS

'As soon as he [Gerrard] opens them legs he's unstoppable to stay with.'
PHIL NEVILLE

'When you see him [Gareth Bale] open his legs like that, it's a fantastic sight.'
GARY NEVILLE

'They have more legs than us.'
DIDIER DROGBA

LAWRENSON

'It must have been like the Alamo. Whatever the Alamo was like.'

    MARK LAWRENSON

'Correct me if I'm not mistaken, John.'

    MARK LAWRENSON

'Patrick Vieira has the best job in the Western Universe.'

    MARK LAWRENSON

'I'm joining you from the paddock here where two horses were accidentally electrocuted… Today we have three more live races for you.'

    ALICE PLUNKETT

'We were lucky that a more serious incident wasn't averted.'

    JOHN FRANCOME

'Tony McCoy looks between his legs and sees Richard Johnson hard at work.'

    AT THE RACES

HOCKEY

'And so for the moment the Great Britain ladies'
hockey team is down to ten men.'

BBC TV

HORSES

'He's twelve months older now than he was twelve
months ago.'

DEREK THOMPSON

'I've never understood players who say, "I no longer want to play international football." It's like saying, "I don't want to play for my country."'

 GRAHAM TAYLOR

'The lack of communication seems non-existent.'

 GRAHAM TAYLOR

'It's one of those things that, unless you see it, it's a really easy thing to miss.'

 GRAHAM TAYLOR

'Chelsea don't play enough in what I call the corners of the pitch.'

 GRAHAM TAYLOR

'Scoring has been quite unbelievable today. If you shoot 69 today, you move up the leaderboard, and I have to say in the wrong direction.'

RICHARD BOXALL

'This Korean dresses very flamboyantly, but he can't match John Daly in the trouser department.'

RADIO 5 LIVE

'The clubhouse is a distance from the first tee and the 18th hole. You can't sit in the window and watch Fred bash one off.'

PETER ALLISS

GRAHAM TAYLOR

'Typically English football, given all the foreign players…'

GRAHAM TAYLOR

'I don't think he chose to put it over the bar, but that's where it went.'

GRAHAM TAYLOR

GOLF

'This wind won't make it easier, but it will make it less difficult.'
BERNARD GALLACHER

'On the first tee, talking of beards, is Clare Balding…'
JOHN INVERDALE

'Chelsea trying to recombobulate, if that's the word.'
CONOR McNAMARA

'This year, if you want to win the Premiership, you are going to have to finish above Man United.'
ALAN BRAZIL

FOOTBALL MANAGEMENT

'You can't really win as England manager. Unless you win.'
GARY NEVILLE

'We want to be in the top four at the end of the season. Anything above that is a bonus.'
HARRY REDKNAPP

'We were poor in both thirds of the field.'
TONY PULIS

'We have to reduce our expectations, and we have the players to do it.'
STEVE McCLAREN

'Are City going to win the league? I'm not going to give you a yes or a no. I'm going to give you a straight yes.'

    MIKE SUMMERBEE

There was nothing wrong with his timing, he was just a bit late…'

    MARK BRIGHT

'There's Carlton Cole, whose equaliser put West Ham in front.'

JEFF STELLING

'You think it's going to be that result or vice versa, but it's the opposite.'

STEVE KEAN

'There's always a keen rivalry between Tottenham and Spurs.'

DAVID PLEAT

'Those two goals have really affected Norwich – they've had the wind taken right out of their stomachs.'

ALAN IRWIN

'If Harry Redknapp had said "Go out and play the worst you possibly can," they couldn't have done any better.'

MARK BRIGHT

'They maybe haven't merited the points they've deserved.'

GARY GILLESPIE

'Dicko has just got a goal back for Blackpool, but I don't think it's going to make any difference to the score.'

STEVE MAY

'A reminder that any goals scored in extra time will count.'

JON CHAMPION

'I don't make predictions about the future.'

NEIL DONCASTER

'If he'd had a clear view, I think he would have seen it.'

   GARY NEVILLE

'He's got 19 goals so far this season. One more and he'll have 20.'

GERRY ARMSTRONG

'This game could go either way. Or it could stay exactly as it is now.'

NICK HARRIS

'Chelsea, by their own standards, are underperformancing.'

RAY STUBBS

'Two goals down, Schalke seemed pretty much dead and buried, but they have dug so deep.'

ITV1

'They [Chelsea] are a former shadow of themselves.'

ALAN SHEARER

'He [John Terry] really wears his shirt on his sleeve.'

RAY PARLOUR

'Robert Pires has a nice habit of passing the ball to his own team.'

JAMIE REDKNAPP

'The smiles are on the faces but the butterflies must be jangling for Southampton.'

GABBY LOGAN

'Three words that strike fear into the heart of every Aberdeen fan: "Queen of the South".'

BBC SCOTLAND

'One real chance, and the goalkeeper was excellent on both occasions.'

GERRY ARMSTRONG

'It's almost been like chess on wheels.'

MARTIN KEOWN

'He could have done one of three things. He didn't do either.'

GORDON STRACHAN

'You can't bite your nose off to spite your face.'

PAUL MERSON

'David Luiz is Brazilian or Portuguese or whatever you want to call it.'

JOHN HOLLINS

'If you're going to get in behind Rio Ferdinand, you've got to show him what you've got and then go in hard.'
JAMIE REDKNAPP

'Brighton are going to need a miracle to pull this one back. Which is unlikely.'
ALAN GREEN

'It's like a stone rolling down a hill, gathering more and more moss.'

GRAEME SOUNESS

'Both teams were battling the weather today. It's pouring down and the gale is almost gale-force.'

CRAIG BURLEY

'If people are saying things about you, good or bad, you must be doing something right.'

RIO FERDINAND

'He [Thierry Henry] has achieved so much here, I think he wouldn't have wanted to blotty, er, bloppy his copybook.'
MARTIN KEOWN

'I'm gabberflasted.'
STEVE McMANAMAN

'It was the old past masters versus the new past masters.'
LEE DIXON

'You wouldn't get England nil, Algeria nil at the European Championships.'
MATT SCOTT

'You don't feel the wind here, because the pitch is actually underground.'
SAM MATTERFACE

'…The teenager, Macheda, now 20.'
JOHN MURRAY

'Goalscorers are the cream of the cake.'
PHIL BROWN

'It was common knowledge they didn't get on –
now everybody knows.'
JOHN HARTSON

'Twenty-two goals in 44 matches. That's better
than one goal in every two games.'
JOHN ACRES

'We're on the crest of a slump.'
IAN HOLLOWAY

'Question marks have to be asked of the Valencia
defenders there.'
DAVID PHILLIPS

'Basel have something to die for now and that is
exactly what they're going to do out there.'
DANNY MILLS

'He's always had a terrific punch in that left foot.'
ALISTAIR MANN

'The ink on the Gary Cahill Chelsea contract isn't
dotted yet.'
STEVE BOWER

'They [Manchester City] can just take their foot off the handbrake, it's so frustrating.'
   ALAN SMITH

'There really is hope for optimism for Man City fans.'
   CHRIS KAMARA

'They've picked up… is it 14 points out of a possible seven? That's superb form.'
   GERRY ARMSTRONG

'John Terry has had more central defensive partners than Fred Astaire.'
JOHN RICHARDSON

'I don't think he was aware that he had a little bit more room than he thought.'
ANDY TOWNSEND

'I've just watched the replay and there is absolutely no doubt – it's inconclusive.'
GARTH CROOKS

'Dimitar Berbatov doubles his goal tally in the league this season from one to three.'
GUY MOWBRAY

'I need to get my ass into gear and pull my finger out.'
FRANK LAMPARD

'And the referee doesn't batter an eyelid.'
TALKSPORT

'In football slang it was a David and Goliath clash.'
MARK AUSTIN

'I can only think of a number of cases using the fingers on less than one hand.'
GORDON TAYLOR

'We're making sure we are not the team with the banana skin on top of our heads.'
DANNY WILSON

'All players want to do well for their country and win an international medal and… erm… I'm not the same.'

ASHLEY COLE

'There's one thing City always lacked, and that's inconsistency.'

RICKY HATTON

'They were outnumbered numerically.'

GARRY BIRTLES

'So many chances being squandered – is that the right adjective to use?'

GABBY LOGAN

'Not one of the Arsenal players surrounded the referee.'

ALAN SHEARER

'That'll dampen the half-time cup of tea.'

CRAIG BURLEY

'It was an abject lesson in finishing.'

MICK McCARTHY

'A total lack of disrespect from the player.'
GARTH CROOKS

'You cannot underestimate how big this game is tonight.'

GARETH SOUTHGATE

'I don't think he'll pay too much lack of respect to them.'

IAIN DOWIE

'That was never a penalty in a million planets.'

ALAN McINALLY

'And here's Drogba again, but the movement's all a bit pedantic.'
MIKE INGHAM

'Ryan Giggs is two years older than he was two years ago.'
CLAYTON BLACKMORE

'Japan and Japanese football goes into hysterical meltdown.'
GUY MOWBRAY

'The crowd are audibly incandescent.'
PETER DRURY

'The manager needs to work an oracle.'
RAY HOUGHTON

'Armand Traore at right back is having a holocaust at the moment.'
TONY CASCARINO

'Swansea, very nearly victims of their own downfall.'
STEVE BOWER

'There are times now when the missing Madrid player is very visible.'
PETER DRURY

'We've seen great European football this season at White Hart Lane – both home and away.'
HARRY REDKNAPP

'It's an unprecedented precedent.'
CLARK CARLISLE

'He is an American, qualified to play for Wales because he has a Welsh grandmother, who was on the bench against Switzerland.'
  GUY MOWBRAY

'London is up there with Madrid or Milan, but Glasgow's unique, along with Liverpool and Newcastle.'
  GEORGE GRAHAM

'People call it Armageddon, but I think it's worse than that.'
  TERRY BUTCHER

'Wrexham just need to match Tamworth's work-rate and then, with their additional quality, the scum will rise to the top.'

KEVIN RATCLIFFE

'Rangers will face disciplinary action from UEFA following alleged secretarian singing…'

ALEX HAMMOND

'On a serious note, though: Fernando Torres has won the World Cup, he's won the European Championships, but he's never won anything as a player.'

DAN WALKER

'He's obviously hurting. You could see that in the tone of his voice.'

ROY KEANE

'When you're comfortable, and you think you're comfortable, it's uncomfortable.'

ROY KEANE

'The boy McLean. He's been like a fresh of bread air since he's come into the team.'

ROY KEANE

'Marseille have reached this stage after losing their first two games without conceding.'
PETER DRURY

'Olsson, weaving his way through the West Brom defence like butter...'
ROBBIE SAVAGE

'They need a couple of players. Maybe even two.'
   CHRIS WADDLE

'Sometimes the pendulum swings both ways…'
   KEVIN KEEGAN

'[Arteta] lurking on the edge of the box… looking for any droppings…'
   DAVID PLEAT

'If I was me, I would pick Lampard…'
RAY PARLOUR

'His entire family are Sheffield United fans. Only his father isn't.'
FOX SOCCER CHANNEL

'The Auld Firm game is a one-off. There are seven of them this season.'
CHARLIE NICHOLAS

'But I can assure anybody out there that my passion for football is second to anybody.'
RAY WILKINS

'If that was outside the box, I don't think that would have been a penalty.'
RAY WILKINS

'Yeah, but two rights don't make a wrong…'
DWIGHT YORKE

'They [Chelsea] could, on another day, have lost today.'
STEVE WILSON

'Didier Drogba's had malaria, so he's not a hundred percent fit for whatever reason…'
GLENN HODDLE

'It's not about tomorrow for Arsenal. It's about the future.'
MICKY QUINN

'Beckham is no rocket surgeon…'
PADDY O'CONNELL

'Nothing's black or white in our country – you're either brilliant or you're hopeless.'
ALAN SHEARER

'A talking goalkeeper is a big asset.'
JIM BEGLIN

'He's got brains on his feet and eyes in the back of his dead!'
DAVID PLEAT

'He hit that ball unerringly past the post.'
DAVID PLEAT

'Whatever ebb and flow means, this is it!'
DAVID PLEAT

'I was particularly pleased with the way we conceded a goal…'
PAUL TISDALE

'Football is a democracy. There's always a dictator at the top.'
DAVID PLEAT

'The goalkeeper mishandled it with both feet.'
NIGEL WORTHINGTON

'There's Fabio Capello, fresh from spending yesterday globe-trotting around the north-west of England.'
SKY TV

'There are some heads spinning in white shirts out there.'

CLIVE TYLDESLEY

'Losing by six goals can certainly take the steam out of your sails.'

RAY WILKINS

'Well, we're not out of the woods yet, but we can see the trees.'

BLACKBURN ROVERS ONLINE

'A cliché to me is like a red rag to a bull.'
PAT NEVIN

'When the chips are down, the top dogs usually come up smelling of roses.'
NEIL WARNOCK

'Gallas might not be accepted at Spurs due to the stigmata attached to him being ex-Arsenal captain…'
CALLER, Radio 5 Live

'We can rattle anyone's feathers.'
MICHAEL OWEN

'We want to raise the bar of the grass roots.'
SIR TREVOR BROOKING

'He couldn't hit the old proverbial with a barn door.'
IAN PAYNE

'[Dzeko] accused of throwing his bathwater out of the pram.'
JAMES COOPER

'There's worries about the position of his groin at the moment.'

    CLIVE TYLDESLEY

'The thing about Drogba is that he scores when he doesn't even play, if that's possible.'

    IAN WRIGHT

FOOTBALL

'It was such a good shot that even if the keeper had saved it, it would have gone in the back of the net.'
LES FERDINAND

'This lance had to be boiled.'
JOHN TERRY

'I'm not sure they deserve it but Wigan have equalised three minutes before the end of time…'
RADIO 5 LIVE

'There's lots of things I inherited from my parents. They both sadly passed away. I've been keeping them in cupboards.'
   CASH IN THE ATTIC

'It's the fourth film in the trilogy!'
   LUCY COTTER

'If it wasn't for my father, I might not be sitting here today.'
   MARIELLA FROSTRUP

DAYTIME

'I want six bridesmaids. You only get married once.'

KATIE PRICE

'And the fleet that defeated Napoleon at Waterloo was built right here, at Chatham.'

MATT BAKER

'This house is crammed with space.'

MARTIN ROBERTS, Homes Under The Hammer

'If my dad were still alive today, he'd turn in his grave.'

JEREMY KYLE SHOW

'Your CV reads like a who's who of what you've done.'

JAMES MARTIN

'Some might think she's [Meryl Streep] won a whole brace of Oscars. In fact she's won only two.'

ALASTAIR LEITHEAD

CYCLING

'Charteau could be tickling the rear end of Moreau if he makes to the top in time.'

CHRIS BOARDMAN

'This man could be the crown in their jewel over the next couple of years.'

PAUL SHERWEN

'Mark Cavendish, the man from the Isle of Man. The man with three legs…'

PHIL LIGGETT

'The ball's on the other foot.'
GRAEME SWANN

'The thing about the triangular series is that whoever wins is the winner.'
TONY GREIG

'Here comes Kohli, chomping at the bat to get in.'
PHIL TUFNELL

'He [D'Oliveira] was a social animal; in fact he was rather like a leopard. After two or three pints, he'd change his spots.'
GEOFFREY BOYCOTT

'I cannot underestimate how well Cook has batted.'
JONATHAN AGNEW

'They've got to get him out quickly, because if they don't he'll stay in'
GEOFFREY BOYCOTT

'Henry Blofeld's looking at his iPad through gritted teeth'
JONATHAN AGNEW

'There aren't many stewards about – you could count them on the fingers of one hand. There are six of them.'

JONATHAN AGNEW

'I'd like to welcome Makhaya Ntini to the commentary box, but you won't be able to see him as we don't have a microphone.'

ROBIN JACKMAN

'The clouds are cloudy.'
    HENRY BLOFELD

'We've just heard Andrew Strauss give Jimmy Anderson the nod.'
    MICHAEL ATHERTON

'It's refreshing to see a bowler run in at 70 miles per hour and swing the ball both ways.'
    BOB WILLIS

'It's time the umpires took the bit by the scruff of the neck.'
    PHIL TUFNELL

'I just said that in exactly the same but different words.'

  GEOFFREY BOYCOTT

'Two of the England cricket team have gone down with stomach disorders. Over now to Jonathan Trott…'

  RADIO 5 LIVE

'It's a bit like unlocking the door to find the horse has bolted.'

  HENRY BLOFELD

CRICKET

'I can't remember a start like this in living memory.'
>   *CHARLES COLVILE*

'The Pakistanis have a natural ability to commit suicide.'
>   *SIMON HUGHES*

'From 150 metres away you'd feel like putting your finger up yourself.'
>   *IAN CHAPPELL*

'Johnson, with two bouncing balls, has got two wickets.'
>   *JIM MAXWELL*

'The wheel goes round, and this time it's on the other foot.'
>   *GEOFFREY BOYCOTT*

'You had to be born for a long time to play for Yorkshire.'
>   *GEOFFREY BOYCOTT*

'All this talk about ripping people's heads off –
that's going below the belt, really.'
MICKY CANTWELL

'I don't know why everybody gives Audley
[Harrison] such a bad press… he's never hurt
anybody.'
GARRY RICHARDSON

BOXING

'He's more underestimated than a lot of people give him credit for.'
FRANK BRUNO

'And now he [Klitschko] has a cut under his left nose…'
LENNOX LEWIS

'It was a war of nutrition tonight.'
KELL BROOK

'It's good to hear the union jack being played at the European Championships.'
   BRENDAN FOSTER

'Phillips Idowu has qualified for the final of the triple jump with a single leap.'
   RADIO NORFOLK

'He's running faster and faster: 4.42, 4.42, 4.47, 4.44…'
   BRENDAN FOSTER

'You were pretty cool at the finish line. Did you know from the start that that was where it was going to end?'
   LOUISE MINCHIN (to hurdler Dai Greene)

'Coached by the very best hurdles coach, if not in this country, certainly in the world.'
   PAUL DICKENSON

BOWLS

'He must be decimated!'
   COMMENTATOR, BBC2

ATHLETICS

'He's [Christophe LeMaitre] really set the gauntlet that everyone's going to try and achieve.'
   COLIN JACKSON

'If you're not out of trouble, you're in trouble.'
   IWAN THOMAS

'He ran so fast the French letters are hanging off.'
   IWAN THOMAS

INTRODUCTION

This is the 16th collection of Commentatorballs, or 'Colemanballs' as it was called until the retirement of Barry Fantoni, its creator and long-time compiler. The change was also due because several generations of Britons had grown up without the faintest idea who David Coleman might have been. (Or, for that matter, Ron Pickering.)

The vast profusion of television channels now means a vast profusion of commentators, summarisers, newsreaders and blank-eyed TV chefs who haven't the slightest idea what they just said, or how silly it made them sound. But this agglomeration of gaffes uttered by the professionals also demonstrates the continuing health and vibrancy of speech radio: in particular Radio 5 Live, the first and so far only radio station explicitly set up to keep the Commentatorballs column going. Not for the first time, football provides by far the largest proportion of the entries used, and three of the sport's more opaque sages have been given sections of their own.

Somewhere, from within these words, meaning is struggling to get out, and failing miserably. Thanks to Simon Edmond, who compiles Commentatorballs for the magazine, and everyone else who contributed.

COMMENTATORBALLS

EDITED BY
MARCUS BERKMANN

ILLUSTRATED BY
ROBERT THOMPSON